PASSING SHOTS

PASSING SHOTS

Words by Catherine Bell
Pictures by Roy Peters

Frederick Muller Limited
London

First published in Great Britain in 1983 by Frederick Muller
Limited, Dataday House, Alexandra Road, Wimbledon,
London SW19 7JZ.

British Library Cataloguing in Publication Data

Bell, Catherine
   Passing shots.
    1. Tennis   2. Athletes
   I. Title
   796.342   GV995
ISBN 0-584-11051-0

Printed in Italy by Arnoldo Mondadori Editore, Verona

The pictures are dedicated to my father.

R.P.

Foreword

The idea for this book grew out of several years observing and writing about tennis – we wanted to see how black and white photography could be used to explain a highly individualistic sport. This book is not meant to be a coaching manual or an exhaustive collection of star portraits: it's simply the way we see tennis in the early 1980s.

R.P.
C.J.B.
October 1982.

Players

Bjorn Borg
Sweden *Wimbledon 1981*

Alone, Bjorn Borg changed the way tennis was played during
the 1970s.

He didn't invent topspin, and he wasn't the first player to use
a double-handed grip, but no man before him had used either
of these techniques to such effect.

Here, Borg is hitting his two-handed backhand on the Centre
Court at Wimbledon. Experts said his style could never adapt
to grass, which is slippery and makes the ball bounce low, but
Borg won Wimbledon five times between 1976 and 1980,
proving that for a man of genius the surface only exists to be
subdued.

All Borg's wizardry is in this picture. Precise footwork has
brought him into a perfect position to meet the ball early; the
high, straight backswing will allow him to hit up and over the
ball with heavy spin and good disguise.

His concentration is perfect. Those close-set eyes in a
somewhat beaky face give away his secret weapon. Many other
tennis players have copied his style; no one can share the
rigorous application of his mind.

Around his neck and on his wrist Borg wears the gold chains
which are obligatory personal adornment for the modern male
tennis professional, but on court he is without frivolity,
immune to distraction. He became richer faster than anyone
else in tennis history, but he remained the essential Puritan.

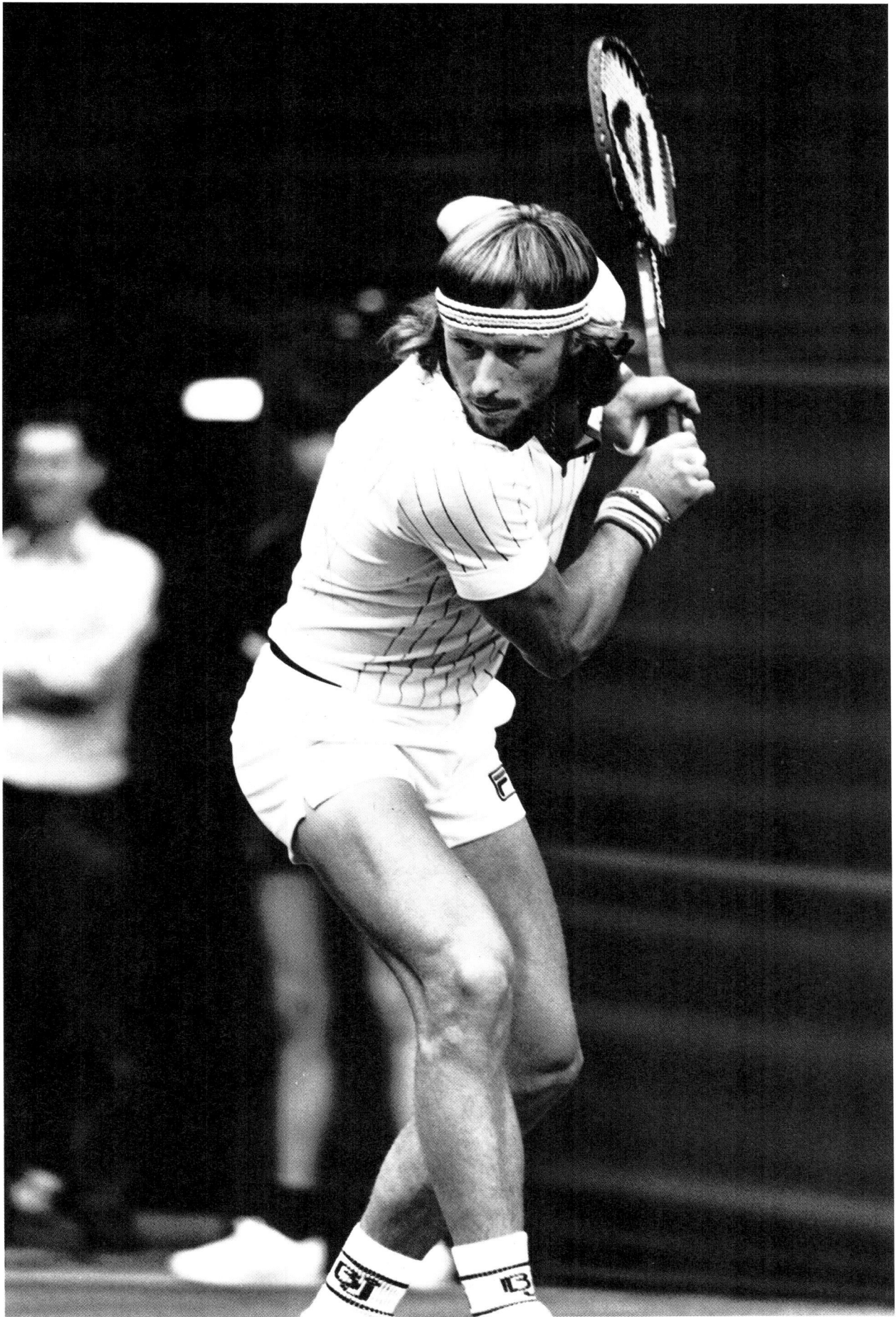

Bjorn Borg
Sweden *Wimbledon 1981*

Borg hasn't missed the ball here. He's swung it away and
closed his eyes. The power of impact and the need for balance
has detached his left hand from the racket; his legs are caught
half way into that step which will bring him around on the
baseline to see what's happened to his shot and to prepare for
a reply.
Although Borg's eyes are shut he's always known where the
ball is.
This picture shows very clearly the points in Borg's physique
which made him the ideal tennis player; broad shoulders,
muscles bursting out of his shirt on his serving arm, narrow
hips, perfectly muscled legs. He walked around the court
with an oddly rolling gait, like a sailor constantly adjusting to
a pitching deck.
Borg's racket, turned as a knife, was made for him by the
Donnay company in Belgium. It has a high leather grip, for
two hands, and is strung for Borg to an incredible tightness.
The ball flies off the strings at great speed with an electronic
ping.
In 1982, after fifteen years of constant tennis, Borg left the
game, suddenly. He never publicly discussed his troubles, he
never complained. He simply became indifferent. The mastery,
the elemental dominance, will never come back.
Bjorn Borg exhausted his loyalty to tennis; anything in the
future must be just for fun.

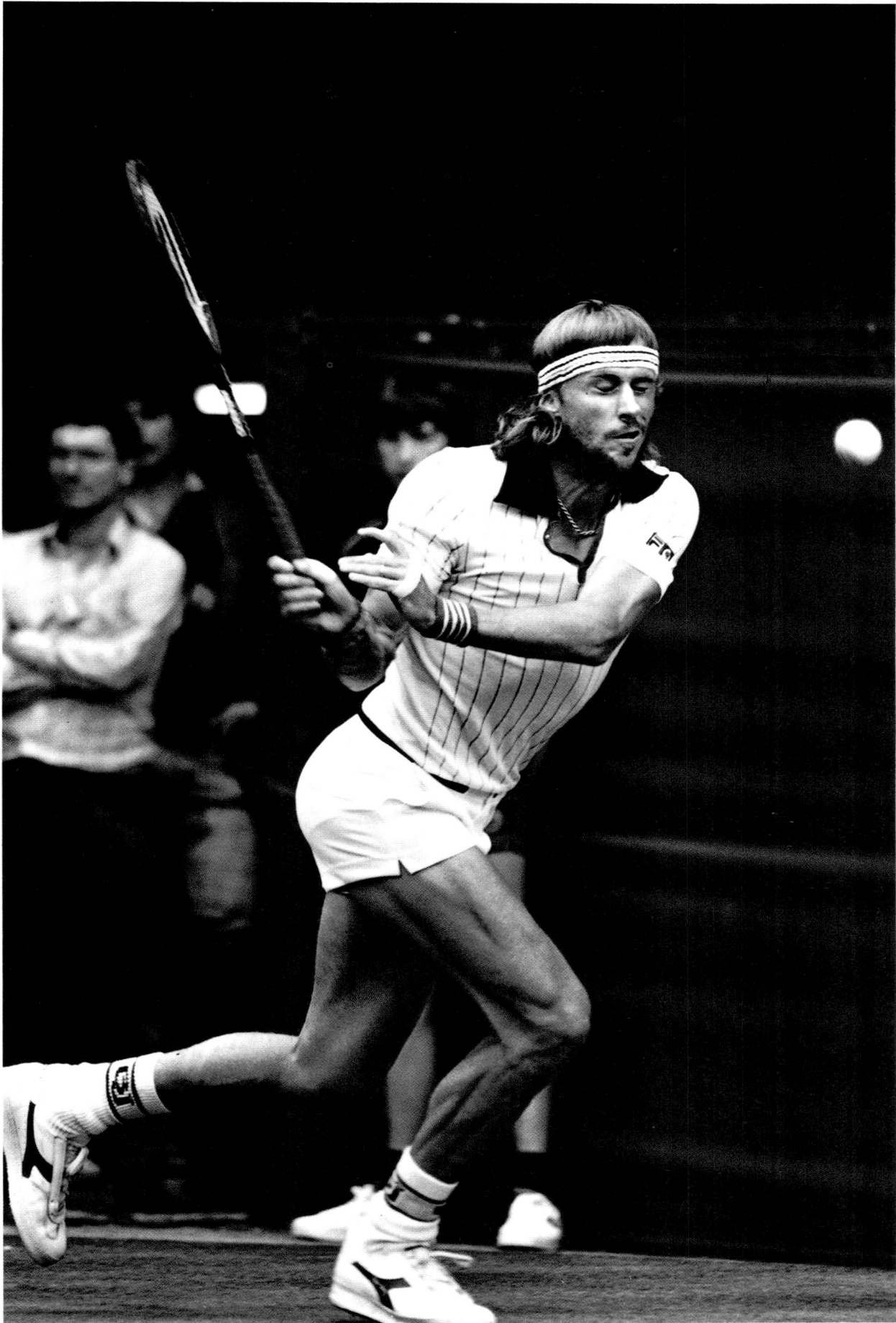

Chris Lloyd
United States *Wimbledon 1982*

Everything is excluded from this portrait of Mrs Lloyd.
There's no ball, no racket, no sense of place. It's difficult even
to say which stroke is about to be played. This is the most
abstract tennis picture.

Chris is shorn of glamour, nearly the pure athlete that part of
her always wanted to be. Her hair's damped down with sweat,
her face is boyish. The modest earrings are a gesture to
fashion, to the well-groomed modern woman she'll change
back into in the dressing-room.

Mrs Lloyd looks like herself as a young girl; those wide and
steely eyes would fix an opponent and will the victory. For
several years almost all women players were afraid of her.

Growing up as a famous person Chris developed a personality
at once reserved and sociable, vulnerable and calculating,
introspective yet immediately affable. She can express a
cynical wit, and in the next breath, a cosily conventional
sentimentality.

She likes to be called "Chrissie", an incongruously dainty
name for a woman so fundamentally tough.

Tennis is a game of recurring crises – again and again you'll
see this fearful look in a player's eyes as the future hangs on a
split second and all will be lost, or won.

Here, the camera has found absolute stillness. That tingling
moment is caught forever.

Chris Lloyd
United States *Wimbledon 1982*

Chris invented this backhand drive.

Her position calls to mind golf, or cricket. Her balance is
perfect – right leg braced against the body rotation, follow-
through high and controlled. Unlike Jimmy Connors or Borg,
Chris doesn't release her left hand at any time during the shot.
This is because her whole manner of execution is more static,
and there's no room for improvisation in movement.

Mrs Lloyd usually dictates the tempo of play so well that she
is seldom caught having to change her mind at the last minute,
so a gallery of stills will show her hitting exactly the same
stroke thousands of times over.

When she was a teenager, skinny and with no figure to speak
of, Chris would wear flouncy skirted dresses and pirouette into
her backhand like a twirling figure on a music-box. As she
grew and matured, that particular freedom was lost although
the fluidity and discipline remained. Chris won many
tournaments because her backhand was absolutely reliable;
she learned new strokes and different strategies but it was
always there to fall back on.

Every great champion has a certain way of hitting the ball
which is a signature. This is how Chris signed herself into
history.

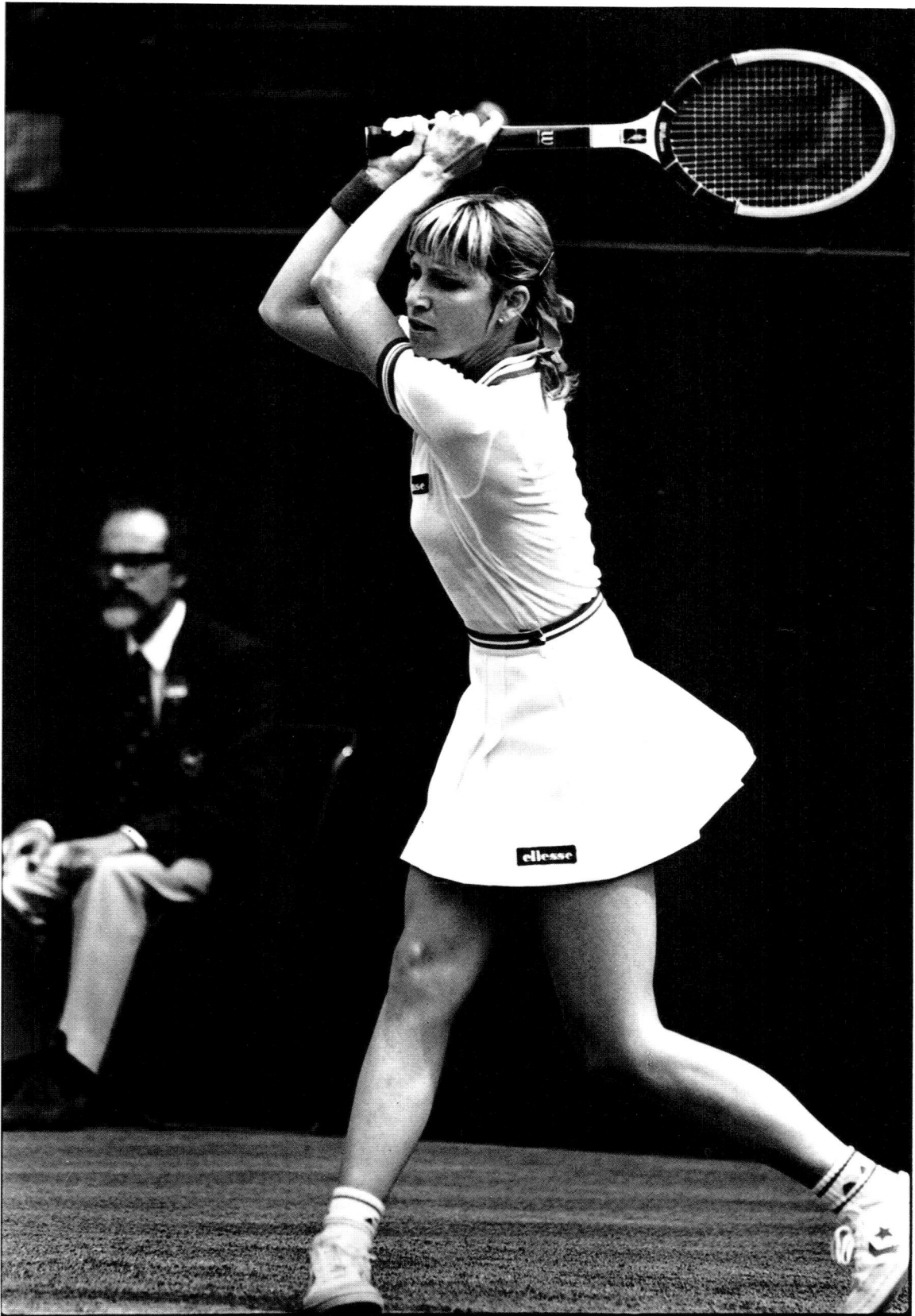

Chris Lloyd
United States *Wimbledon 1981*

Chris is studying a drop-shot. The spectators are studying
Chris.
Mrs Lloyd's careful tennis inspires thoughtfulness in crowds,
and decorous appreciation.
The drop-shot is a teasing, sadistic ploy, dependent on bluff,
duplicity and icy nerves.
The drop-shot became, after her ground strokes, Chris's
speciality. She will twitch her opponent about the court then
tip the ball over the net, just so, and leave her victim stranded.
A winning drop-shot always means humiliation for the loser.
Mrs Lloyd, no mean psychologist, recognised the demolition
value of embarrassment.
Here, she's close to the net and inside the service line, hitting a
classic forehand with underspin, body compactly poised and
translating into action the precise intention of her mind. There
is a certain courage, too, for the drop-shot will bring its best
reward when the risks are highest.

Jimmy Connors
United States *Wimbledon 1981*

Jimmy is throwing himself at the ball very much as he threw
himself at tennis.

He won Wimbledon for the first time in 1974 and for the
second time in 1982. In between he didn't change a bit.

Jimmy grew up in East St Louis, Illinois, an ordinary
proletarian background a million miles from establishment
East Coast America or sunburnt California. He always carried
a kind of chip on his shoulder because of that. In many
countries you would call it class distinction, but in the land of
the free Jimmy's belligerence has to be put down to motives
like momism or sheer bloody-mindedness.

Connors learned tennis from his mother and grandmother, and
the fact was only made much of because, as a man, this looked
kind of sissy. He was once said to be the best man playing
women's tennis.

In fact Jimmy Connors plays tennis the way every champion
has – he found a style natural to him early in life and stuck
to it.

He hits the ball hard and flat, and he never tires of hitting it.
His forehand was always terrible, for a champion, but Jimmy
wins anyway.

He is completely faithful to his racket. This is the Wilson
T2000 – a miracle of aluminium and trampolining strings
which went out of fashion among professional tennis players
around 1970.

Jimmy's control and timing is such that in his hands this
racket has become an instrument.

Look at Jimmy's fingers. For an athlete they are unusually fine.
His hair flies outwards, his body contorts. Yet in the midst of
all this mayhem there is delicacy, and touch.

Jimmy Connors
United States *Paris 1982*

Connors is enduring (even hesitantly enjoying) that strange by-product of modern professional tennis, the Post-Match Interview.

For these, a player who has done all his speaking on the tennis court with the tools he knows best, is brought before a group of journalists, ranging in style from quality to gutter, and required to recreate a match which all of them should have watched anyway.

The Interview developed because many tennis reporters don't understand the game and need the Quote. The Quote provides the lead story on any match. The Quote, for many reporters, is indispensable. Without it, tennis writing would be a matter of service breaks and game scores. The Quote is human interest.

Players react to the Interview in different ways. Those who are very young may find they are subtly being asked to define their own sense of self through this relationship with the press. Growing up becomes public.

Jimmy Connors progressed to adulthood in tennis via the press room, and to an accommodation with reporters which could be called amicably hostile. He's at ease with himself and can joke or be tough. He can play-act or be absolutely serious in dissecting his performance.

But the Interview generally only increases a feeling in the press room that reporters and players are locked together in some media fandango, and neither dances the same step.

Good Interviews come from players who know the rules – Jimmy, Chris Lloyd, Billie Jean King, Pam Shriver.

Sometimes a player cracks, pain and confusion spill out, and the nasty, the voyeuristic nature of sports reporting shows itself.

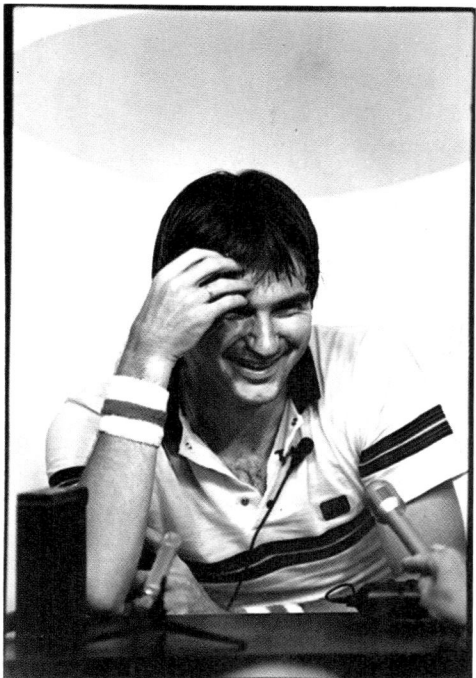

Jimmy Connors
United States   *Wimbledon 1982*

Grass flies where Connors' silver racket scrapes the ground in this desperate lunge. He's hit a defensive lob retrieve, slicing the ball so it hovers in the air, and he has time to recover himself and charge back into the fray.
Winning comes from never giving up, from chasing balls into the back netting, falling over, *getting the ball back*.
Jimmy's glance over his shoulder tells him this pursuit was successful; the ball is in court, the point goes on, the game is still to be played for.

Martina Navratilova
United States *Wimbledon 1982*

Miss Navratilova is on her way out of the Centre Court after beating Chris Lloyd and winning her third Wimbledon singles title.

She's been temporarily halted by an American television reporter who has thrust a microphone under her nose and asked for instant thoughts on the match.

The flowers are an equivocal intrusion. They remind us that the woman athlete remains a woman first.

Most of her life Martina has been caught in this dilemma, for in every respect but sheer muscle power she plays tennis exactly like a man. Our culture won't give her the freedom to do this unless she makes regular symbolic gestures asserting her femininity. So she dyes her hair blonde, wears make-up, discreet jewellery and smart casual clothes.

Once on the tennis court Miss Navratilova must forget all these gestures and try to win through strength and intimidation.

For a woman player, the path to achievement is an obstacle race past social taboos and inhibitions.

Martina Navratilova can smile here, because the compromises have been made and the championship won.

The logo on her sleeve is the name of a cigarette brand. It is also a tennis clothing line. Cigarette advertising is forbidden on television in Britain. There are other compromises being made here too.

Martina Navratilova
United States *Paris 1982*

Martina has hit a perfect backhand volley cross court, most
probably a winner since her opponent is nowhere in sight.
Of course, because this is Paris and the court surface loose-
topped clay, there can be no certainty that the ball's slow
bounce will not allow time for the player across the net to run
this volley down and slam it away past Martina who is now too
close to the net to do much about a ball behind her.
But this stroke is so efficiently controlled, with no sense of
hurry, that the chances are it will seal the point. Martina has
skidded into the shot, a technique perfected on clay, which
allows for a tastefully-balanced arrangement of arms and legs
pleasing both to the photographer and the player. Her legs are
bent, letting her racket take the ball low and apply some slice
or underspin, and the right arm is outstretched as a
counterweight.
The invention of the long lens allows us practically onto the
court and behind the eyes of the volleyer.
Miss Navratilova grew up on European clay, but for several
years after her defection to the United States in 1975 she
avoided competing there. For a basically attacking player,
Paris can be an unrewarding experience. In 1982, however,
Martina mixed patience with enterprise and won her first
French Open title.

Martina Navratilova
United States *Wimbledon 1982*

Miss Navratilova's concern with her appearance has verged
on narcissism.
Happily, the tennis court's a great reducer of such vanities;
Martina wouldn't carry off any beauty prizes in this pose.
Only players of more stately games can win matches and keep
their mascara dry.

John McEnroe
United States *Wimbledon 1982*

This is John McEnroe as we'll remember him.
Returned to babyhood, he's asking why the world cannot be a perfect place.
His bellow of rage is the sad plaint of an infant: *"It's not fair!"*
Early on in McEnroe's competitive career a kindly umpire should have looked down from his tall chair and simply said: *"Life's* not fair, John."
Meanwhile, tennis officials around the globe are poised, like sprinters breaking from blocks, when McEnroe flickers an eyelid.
During a match John's conscious of everything; he's one of the most distractible players who ever lived. On edge, the slightest thing will enrage him. He wants absolute calm, absolute attention, and he'll ask for it in the most peremptory way.
Tournament tennis is a sport for selfish people because the game requires pre-occupation with one's own performance, one's own state of mind.
During a match, John McEnroe is absorbed solely in the rightness of his cause.
Aware of others, and indifferent to them, he makes selfishness the servant of his talent.

John McEnroe
United States *Wimbledon 1982*

McEnroe is improvising a volley.

His style is no style. It's instantly recognisable, and as hard to grasp as all those dinks and chips he's always hitting.

He dangles the racket, drags the head lower than his wrist, waves it away from his body, jumps at the ball, does all the things you're not supposed to do and has all the boys in the park copying him.

McEnroe makes nonsense of the usual geographic descriptions of grips – Eastern, Western, Continental. He holds the racket whichever way he wants. His grip here is a little higher on the racket handle than textbooks would advise, but this gives him extra feel and flexibility – "wristiness".

In spite of his vocal aggression, John's always been a gentle player, a deflector of volleys and precise placer of ground strokes. Compare his left arm with that of Guillermo Vilas. He's five foot eleven inches tall and weighs around one hundred and sixty-five pounds, but he often gives an impression of frailty. He's prone to injury, a young man whose physical and mental condition is interrelated and finely tuned.

Andrea Jaeger
United States *Birmingham 1982*

Andrea Jaeger, of Swiss and Austrian descent, decked out in
Italian Fila clothes, clutching an American racket, turns from
the net and hitches up her bra strap. A kid, just out of pigtails,
makes an unselfconscious hint at maturity.

The sexuality in this picture is direct and open. The tomboyish
appeal of Miss Jaeger contrasts with a much more complicated
scenario suggested by Kathy Renaldi (qv).

Andrea was a prodigy who arrived on the tournament scene at
the right time to make a killing, financially and competitively.
Her ex-boxer father Roland was very much in the picture; you
never saw Andrea at an important event without Roland. He's
a European father – dominating and pushing. How much
Andrea would have accomplished without him is something
we can guess at.

Andrea Jaeger
United States *Wimbledon 1982*

Andrea is playing on grass, on Wimbledon's Centre Court.
Her body's cramped; the centre of gravity is all wrong.
A player like Andrea who hits with two hands is usually at a
disadvantage on grass for you don't have the mobility and
hence the time to ensure that the ball is exactly where you
want it to be.
The camera doesn't lie – awkwardness is deficiency of
technique.
Miss Jaeger developed her style on American clay, a surface
she understands.
At Wimbledon she's always looked like a kid out of her class.

Ivan Lendl
Czechoslovakia *Paris 1982*

Ivan Lendl resembles a marionette temporarily detached from
the puppet master. He's about to strike his fearsome forehand
on the loose red clay of the Stade Roland Garros.
Only a man of great strength can hold the racket like this.
Lendl's Continental grip almost breaks the wrist coming under
and over a high bouncing ball and whipping it with topspin.
The ball will whirl forward on its return journey across the net
and kick from the court almost to the opponent's eye-level.
Back it will go, back it will come, again and again. The
tortuous surface devours massive talents by a process of steady
chewing – after criss-crossing the baseline hundreds of times
in one rally some very big stars have found their grandiose
dreams distilled to sad little pools of sweat.
Lendl should win Paris : his heavy slogging tennis might have
been invented with Roland Garros in mind. But strange things
happen here – perhaps the sportive little crocodile snapping at
Ivan's calf, the trademark of René Lacoste, is the mischievous
spirit of Gallic anarchy ?
Lendl's personality invites persiflage ; he's proud and
inflexible, a high-cheeked Slav from the industrial heart of
Czechoslovakia. His patience with lesser minds is too often as
short as his haircut.
Justice dictates that this sometimes pompously upright youth
should be caught by the camera in a most ridiculous position.

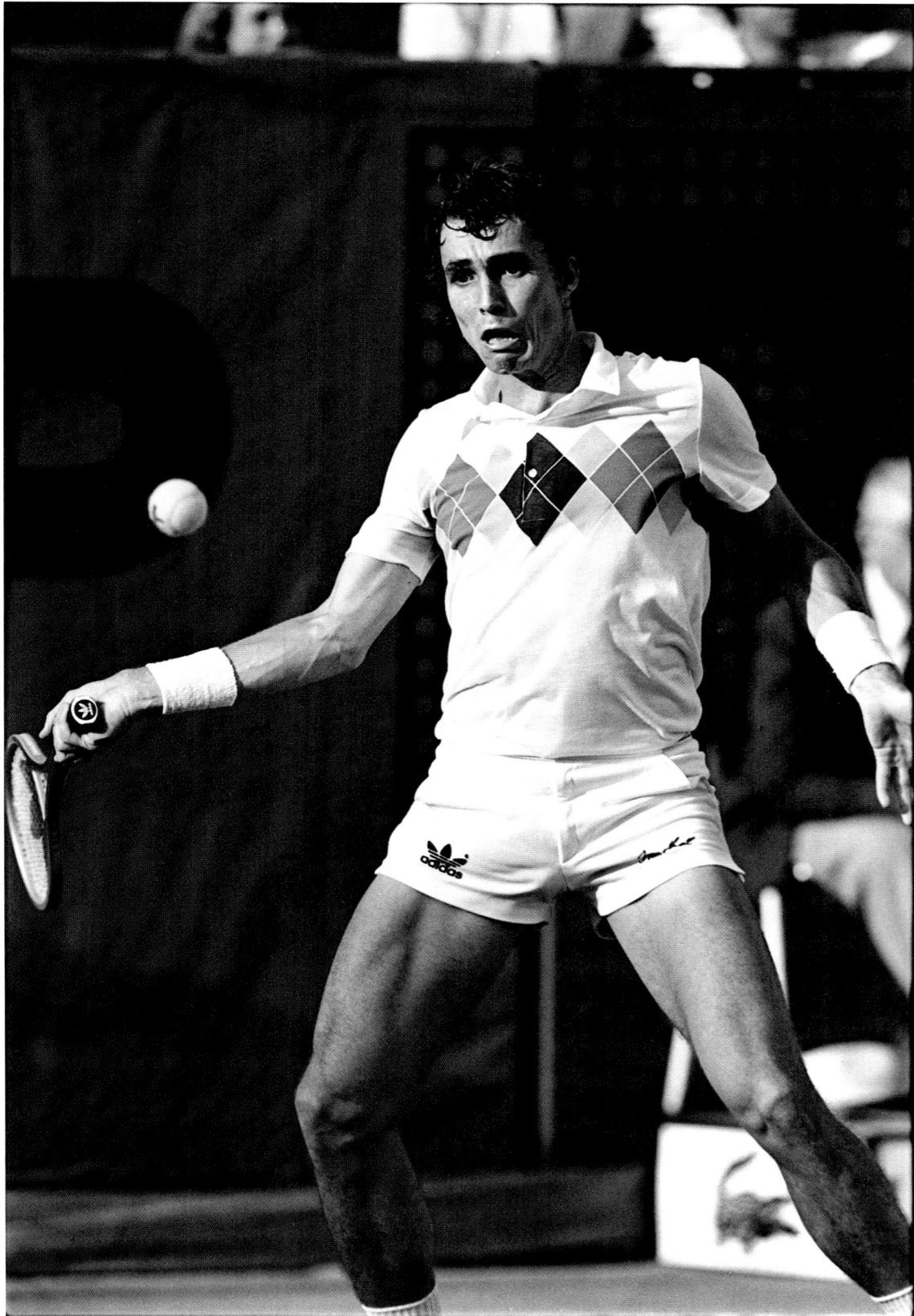

Ivan Lendl
Czechoslovakia *Paris 1982*

Lendl's lifted return of serve reminds us that the backhand is
the freest and most expressive stroke in tennis.
The graceful uncoiling action and use of the striking shoulder
means the ball can be hit with great power and fluency.
Lendl has flung his right arm high and wide, but his body is
almost militarily compact; he's not one for superfluous
movement.
His forehand strikes terror into faint hearts – it wins matches;
but his backhand is the superior shot – it saves them.

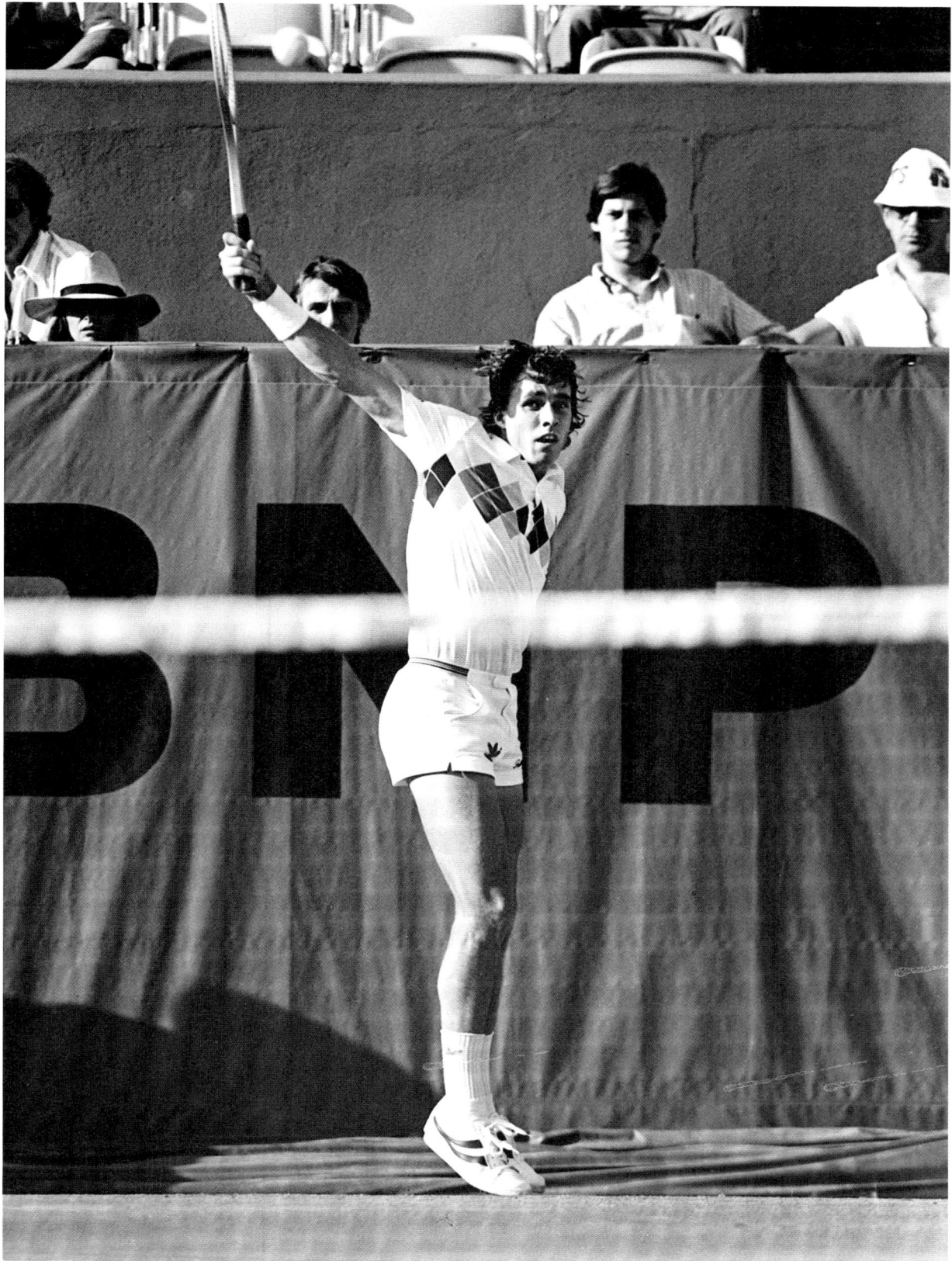

Hana Mandlikova
Czechoslovakia *Paris 1982*

Hana Mandlikova's expression is dubious; so, at this time, was her future.

Hana came from the new generation of Czech players who grew up in the years following Martina Navratilova's defection to the United States. As a youngster she ball-girled for Martina at the Sparta Club in Prague.

Hana modelled her serve and volley style on Martina's example, but she didn't share Miss Navratilova's variety of shot or imperious personality. After some early successes Hana was afflicted with a back injury, then devastating and demoralising losses.

Her place in the game's hierarchy remains problematical.

She's tall, slim, shy, unprovocative; her strokes are graceful, orthodox, evanescent. Her attitude to the strain of competition is often bafflingly placid.

What's going on behind that headband is known to very few.

Tracy Austin
United States *Birmingham 1982*

Tracy more or less grew up falling over a tennis racket; her
family live in sporty, affluent southern California. Two older
brothers and a sister all played the circuit.

Tracy's junior record was the best in American history. She
appeared on the cover of a national magazine when she was
four years old.

As a professional she's never made number one in the world,
and now younger girls look likely to pass her by on the
ranking lists.

Tracy plays basically the same style as Chris Lloyd, but
without her compatriot's flair. Her tactical grasp seems more
limited, her public appeal decidedly so.

This expression of ferocity contrasts oddly with the carefully
tended and polished finger nails.

Tracy has always tried hard to balance her athletic prowess
with the formal demands of femininity in middle America.

Vitas Gerulaitis
United States *Wimbledon 1981*

Vitas was a good American junior whose name nobody could pronounce.

Then he became the rising star, the swinging single, Broadway Vitas.

He played and lost a wonderful semifinal against his friend Bjorn Borg at Wimbledon in 1977, then he did nothing much for a long time.

Vitas seemed to have wanted things easily, both the image and the achievement.

His tennis game is sound, his strokes correct; he runs fast. Why couldn't he win more often?

He's Lithuanian by descent, the product of proud parents who believe in the American Dream because it's done so well by them.

He lives in a nice part of Long Island with a pool and a bedroom with mirrors, and he's bought the obligatory condominium at a posh site in Florida.

Vitas, son of immigrants, arrived.

But this picture, taken during a changeover when he's pausing to towel himself off, suggests conflict in the lives of player and playboy. Sweat, stubble and strain are the other side of long nights and careless days.

Hardly anyone in tennis has really got through to Vitas. He almost always refuses to be interviewed.

The press have left him alone as his talent ebbs and flows.

Evonne Cawley (*née* Goolagong)
Australia *Birmingham 1982*

This is an unusual photograph of Mrs Cawley because she
would appear to have paid some slight attention as to how she
hit the ball.

Mostly Evonne will wave her racket vaguely and let her gaze
drift to a far horizon. She'll give the impression of having
happened on the court by chance.

Her strokes are pure serendipity too; caught in no-man's-land,
bandy-legged, off-balance, she's produced a shot which is still
a marvel of grace and creativity. There could be no better use
of that out-flung left arm, no better illustration of Mrs
Cawley's ability to regard her tennis racket as simply another
part of her body.

Her style is continuous motion; for this reason she's never
photographed particularly well in action. Frozen in frames
you've lost that flowing seamless whole; the inspired
nonconformism just looks weird and slack.

Through the years Mrs Cawley has pursued a professional
career no one changed her tennis and no circumstance was
serious enough to challenge her intermittent attachment to the
game. She won Wimbledon in 1971 at the age of nineteen, and
won it again in 1980. In between she became famous as a
runner-up.

Like most great Australian champions of sport, Evonne
Goolagong came from the country, from the New South Wales
Riverina township of Barellan, and then via Sydney and a bit
of urban polish. Her family were part aboriginal and
uncomplaining rural poor.

Evonne became rich through tennis but she never seemed
encumbered by money or corrupted by the excesses of
professional sport. She didn't get involved and people made
excuses for her because when she played at her best you forgot
about the troubles of the world. Evonne somehow preserved
the spirit of amateurism into the 1980s.

If she were young today there would be no room for her
among the Rinaldis and Austins and Jaegers.

Guillermo Vilas
Argentina *Monte Carlo 1981*

The press, looking for an easy tag, once called Vilas the Mild
Bull of the Pampas, as if this husky son of a well-to-do lawyer
from urban Mar del Plata had somehow spent his youth
roping cattle on the grass plains of Argentina.
He was, nevertheless, an odd addition to the pro tennis ranks.
He wore his hair long, and still does, years after every other
man in the Western world had shorn their locks. He wanted to
be an intellectual, write books and be the Artist as Sportsman,
a curiously old-fashioned idea.
His poetry was never much good (the blind Borges said:
"Imagine me playing tennis!"), his utterances often
pretentious: but Vilas has always been easy to like.
As a player he had a fundamental ball sense and an
extraordinary physique. Look at his left arm.
But he had very little notion of how to win a match.
Competitiveness was not built into his nature. Everything was
work, work.
Vilas is so strong he could work most players off the court,
except those with more brains and equal stamina.
He thinks too much. Jimmy Connors and Bjorn Borg beat him
at vital times because Guillermo was still thinking about what
he should do.
Whatever the stroke, Vilas *heaves* the ball. He has to – he has
nothing else.

Guillermo Vilas
Argentina *Monte Carlo 1981*

Vilas' expression is detached, calm, wistful.
In 1976, finding himself too much alone on the tournament
circuit, Guillermo asked the Rumanian Ion Tiriac to be his
travelling coach, companion and maybe surrogate father. It
was widely believed that Tiriac's main job involved introducing
iron into Guillermo's poetic soul.
In tournaments Tiriac will sit smoking cigarettes by the
courtside, now and again passing hand signals to Vilas, but
mainly just being there. Tiriac refers to himself and Vilas as
"we".
The Rumanian and the Argentinian speak to each other in
Italian when they must use words.
Can Vilas win without Tiriac? Can Vilas even *play* without
Tiriac? This dreamy boy lashing topspin in Monte Carlo is
only half the story.

Kathy Rinaldi
United States *Wimbledon 1981*

Kathy Rinaldi was fourteen years old when this picture was
taken at Wimbledon. She was at that time the youngest player
ever to win a match there, and shortly afterwards she became a
professional. The elderly linesman watching Miss Rinaldi
emphasises the ever more yawning gulf between those who
play tennis and those who judge and administer it.
About to serve, Kathy's caught in a pose where the action of a
sportswoman is given a tantalizingly sexual allure; her routine,
practised and completely casual act of reaching for the ball in
her panties gets an unanticipated erotic force from that
baby-faced pout.
As a double-handed player Miss Rinaldi cannot hold the spare
serving ball in her hand once the point has begun, so she keeps
it under her skirt. Legions of girls with similar styles, barely
pubescent, are advancing into the ranks of women's
professional tennis. Who is watching them and why? This
picture, deliberately voyeuristic, provokes an answer.

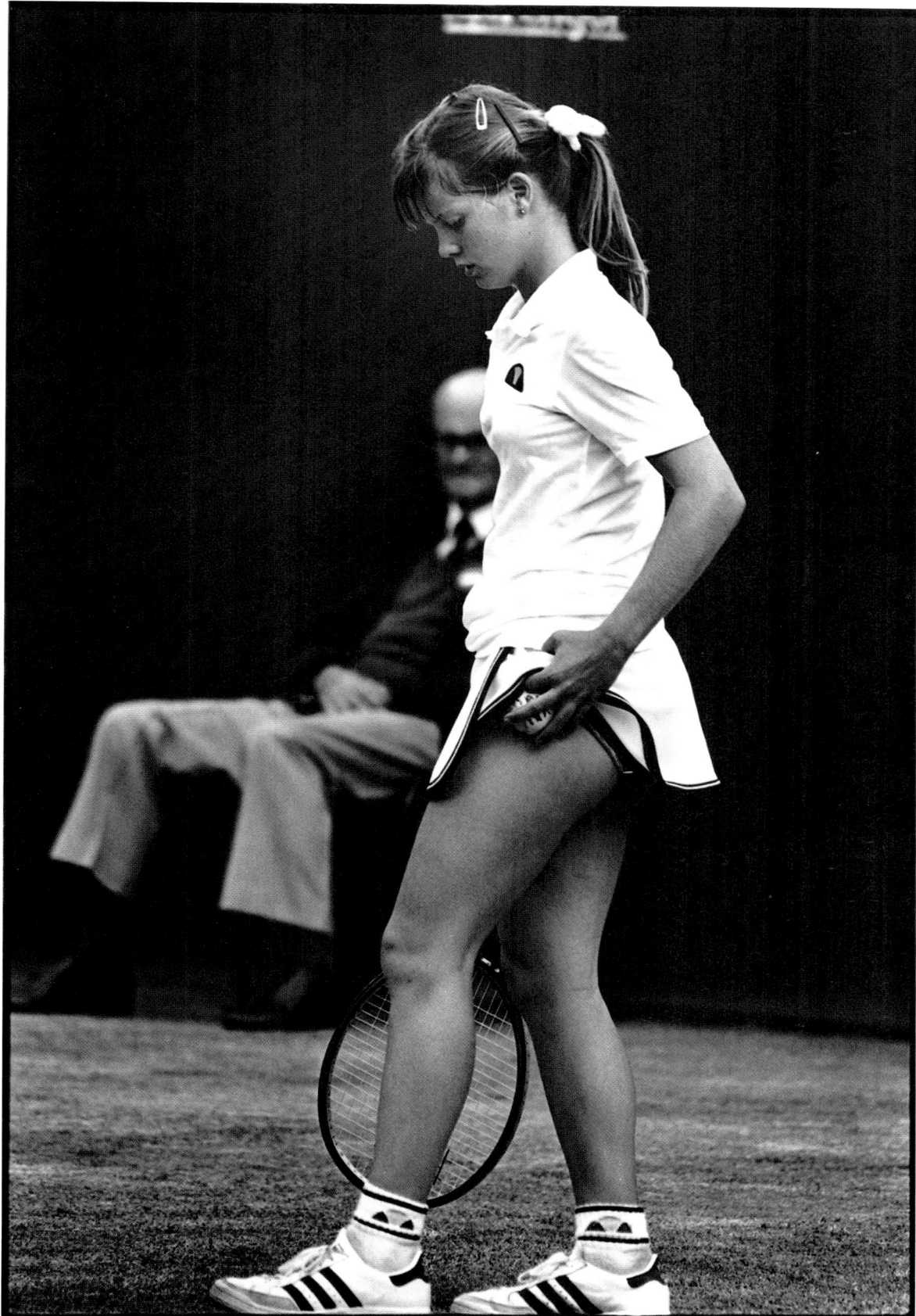

Buster Mottram
Great Britain *Wimbledon 1982*

Buster's private dream is to die on some foreign frontier
wrapped in a Union Jack.
He even plays tennis standing to attention.
Meanwhile, he's wearing Italian shoes and Italian clothes; he
uses an Austrian racket and plays club tennis in West
Germany.
But he turns out regularly for Britain in the Davis Cup where
patriotism has inspired him to a remarkable record of personal
victories.
Other times, he'll tell you that playing tennis is "a joke".
Buster wants to go into Parliament, where he'll sit on the back
benches and rabbit on – a true English eccentric who might
have got swept into competitive tennis entirely by accident.

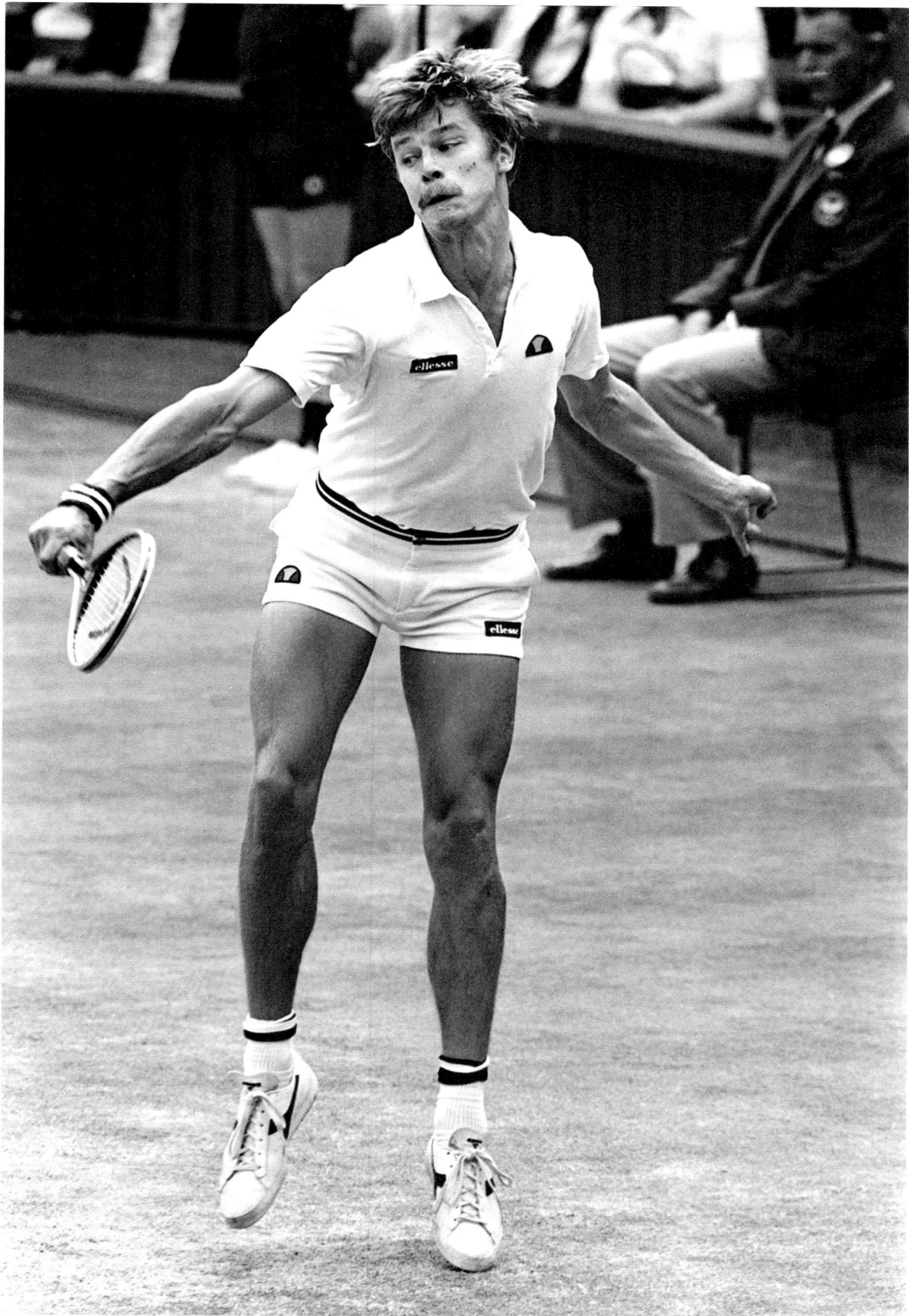

Billie Jean King
United States *Birmingham 1982*

Billie Jean King first competed at Wimbledon in 1961 when
she was seventeen years old. Twenty-one years later she
reached the semifinals there for the thirteenth time.
In between, she went to college, dropped out, married, spent a
summer in Australia re-modelling her backhand, turned
professional with a four woman touring circus, won six
Wimbledon singles titles, four United States singles titles and
innumerable doubles with various partners, pioneered a new and
bigger women's pro circuit, beat Bobby Riggs in straight sets
at the Astrodome in 1973 in front of thirty thousand people,
had an abortion, played tennis and sang on stage with Elton
John, was voted the most admired and influential woman in
America, had her hair permed, failed as a sports magazine
publisher and inter-city league tennis promoter, was operated
on three times for damaged knees, changed the make and
composition of her racket twice, wrote two autobiographies,
retired once, and was sued by her former secretary-lover for
maintenance.
Rosemary Casals nicknamed her the Old Lady.
She is five feet four and a half inches tall and has always
suffered from a tendency to chubbiness. She was severely
short-sighted and often claimed never to have felt entirely well
throughout her competitive career.
Billie Jean's tennis was classical, her strokes copybook. The
knees failed her over the years, the right arm, never.
She's playing here at the Edgbaston Priory Club, Birmingham,
on her favourite surface, grass.
She's flying out for a high forehand volley, striking a ballet
pose. The shoulder and arm muscles are perfectly moulded,
the racket grip high on the handle but firm.
Here you can find strain and symmetry, desperation and control.
Tennis for Billie Jean King was physical adventure between
straight white lines.

60

Billie Jean King
United States *Birmingham 1982*

If all the tennis players who ever lived were wiped from human memory and only Billie Jean King remained, you could reconstruct from the perfection of her technique the complete competitor.

Here Mrs King is running into a backhand volley, her finest shot. Volleying is the heart of aggressive, intelligent tennis, and no one, man or woman, ever volleyed better than Billie Jean, or ever understood so well the aesthetic and tactical possibilities of this beautiful stroke.

Today the arid strategies of topspin have forced everyone back to the baseline and taken away the impulse to move forward. Volleying, for the time being, has vanished from contemporary tennis vocabularies, but as long as Mrs King lives and breathes we can study in her its purest execution.

Billie Jean King
United States *Birmingham 1982*

These scarred and chubby legs must have travelled a million
miles.
They are the most famous legs in tennis.
And then Billie Jean's hands, bouncing the ball before she
serves, remind you that precision is as much part of this game
as power.

Steve Denton
United States   *Wimbledon 1982*

Tennis can be an amazingly becoming sport for human beings
to play, or a spasm of swift and convulsive action.
Steve Denton has, like John McEnroe, improvised a volley,
but Steve's only your average touring pro, not a natural. So
he's tied in knots, startled, pulling his racket away as though
the ball's electric.
Points must be won; only photographers and pseudo-
intellectuals think about appearances.
Denton's a great man for reaction close to the net; with Kevin
Curran of South Africa he's in the top flight of men's doubles.
Alone, in singles, he'll never be more than an inspired finalist.

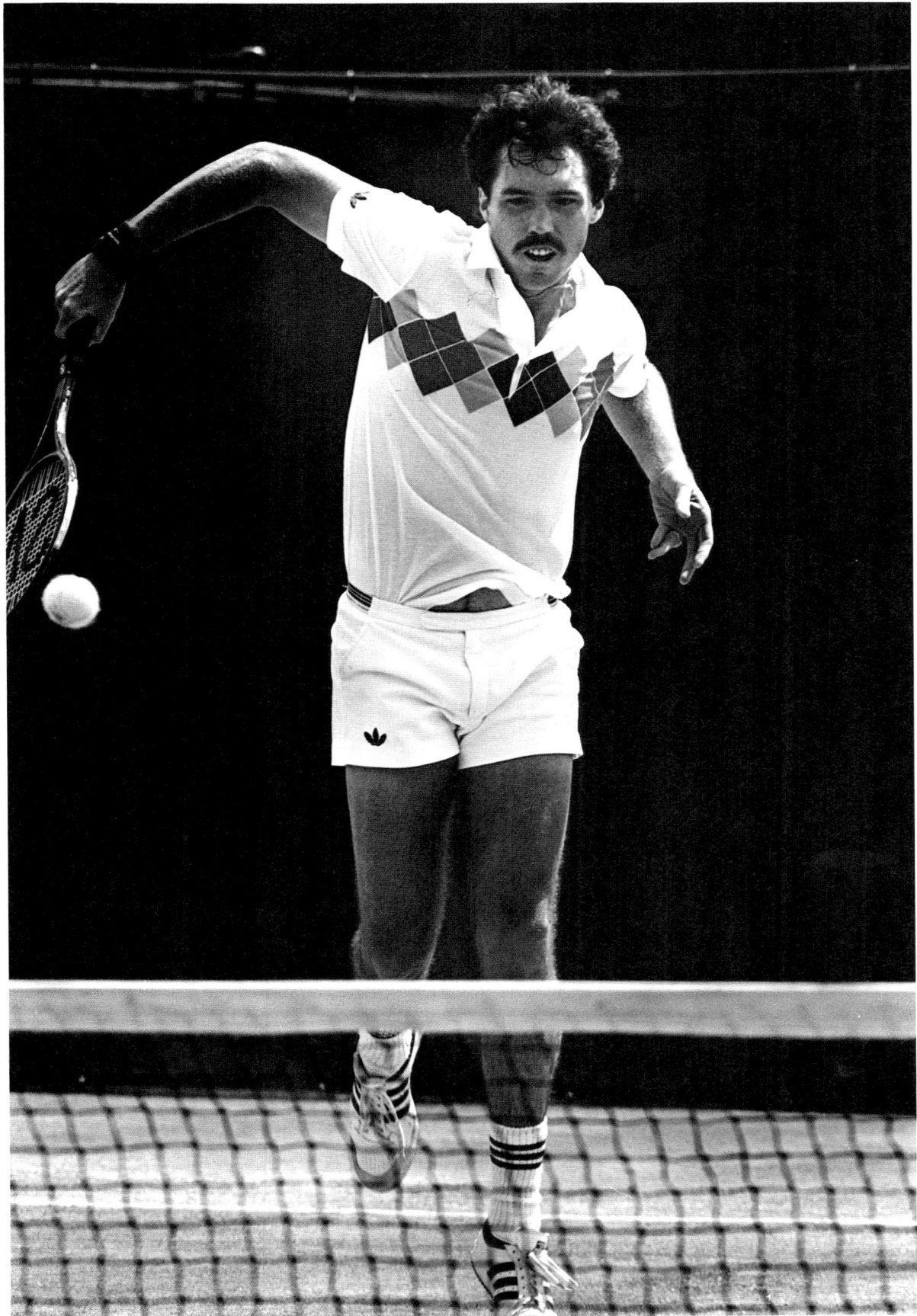

Johan Kriek
South Africa *Bristol 1981*

Kriek is zebra striped, and zebra fast around the court.
He's an Afrikaner who unusually fled South Africa because he
felt left out of things by the tennis establishment.
He followed his coach to Austria and now lives in Florida.
He's jumping for a reflex volley, the kind you hit more out of
fearless hope than certainty, a grass-court shot.
If Kriek learned patience, he'd be more than just a contender.

Bettina Bunge
West Germany *Wimbledon 1982*

Bettina was born in Switzerland and grew up in Peru. Now
she lives in Florida and plays in international competition for
West Germany.

She learned tennis in South America, which is probably why
she's one of the very few girls presently under twenty-one who
doesn't flail away with two hands like something off a coach's
assembly line.

Bettina practises that long lost art – the all-court game. She's
a bouncy, compact player with a nice volley and a generally
optimistic outlook.

On the circuit she hangs out with German girls and isn't
known in the press corps as a great conversationalist.

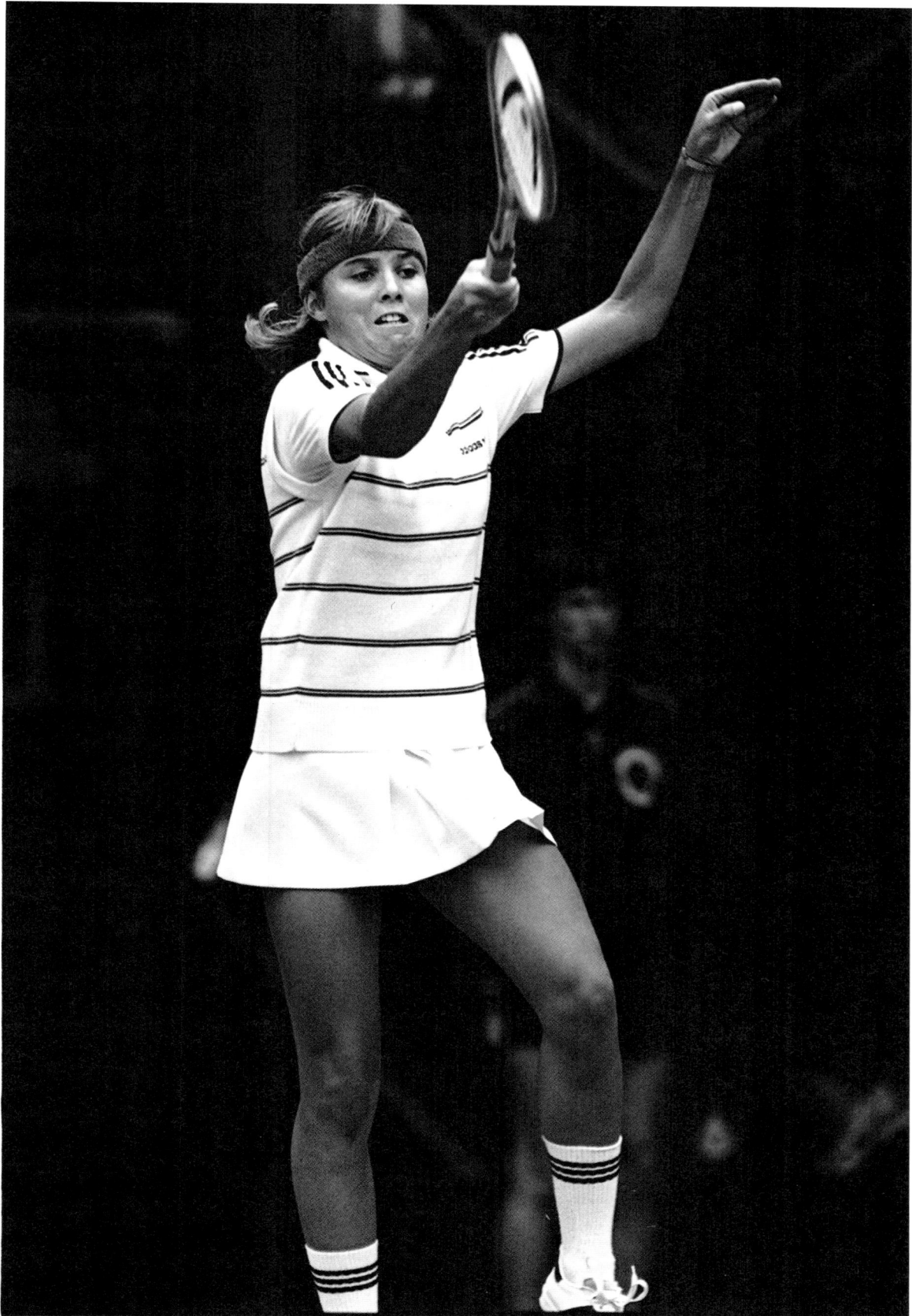

Serves

Vitas Gerulaitis
United States *Wimbledon 1982*

The serve in tennis is a personal stroke, the only time a player
is absolutely unconstrained by the reaction of his opponent.
So it's not surprising everyone develops idiosyncratic ways of
putting a ball in the air and hitting it across the net.
Vitas Gerulaitis has taken such individualism further.
He's become famous for his service *preparation.*
Some players bounce the ball a hundred times and flex their
muscles.
Vitas turns, like a nervous man on a dark city street, to look for
something behind him.
Over the course of a match a wordless bond will grow between
Gerulaitis and the linesmen he turns to.
Is he looking for reassurance, support? Is it a sign of
emotional unease? Amateur psychologists can indulge
themselves.
Whatever the truth, Vitas' touching little practice suggests his
absurdly macho image covers a healthy amount of regular
human vulnerability.

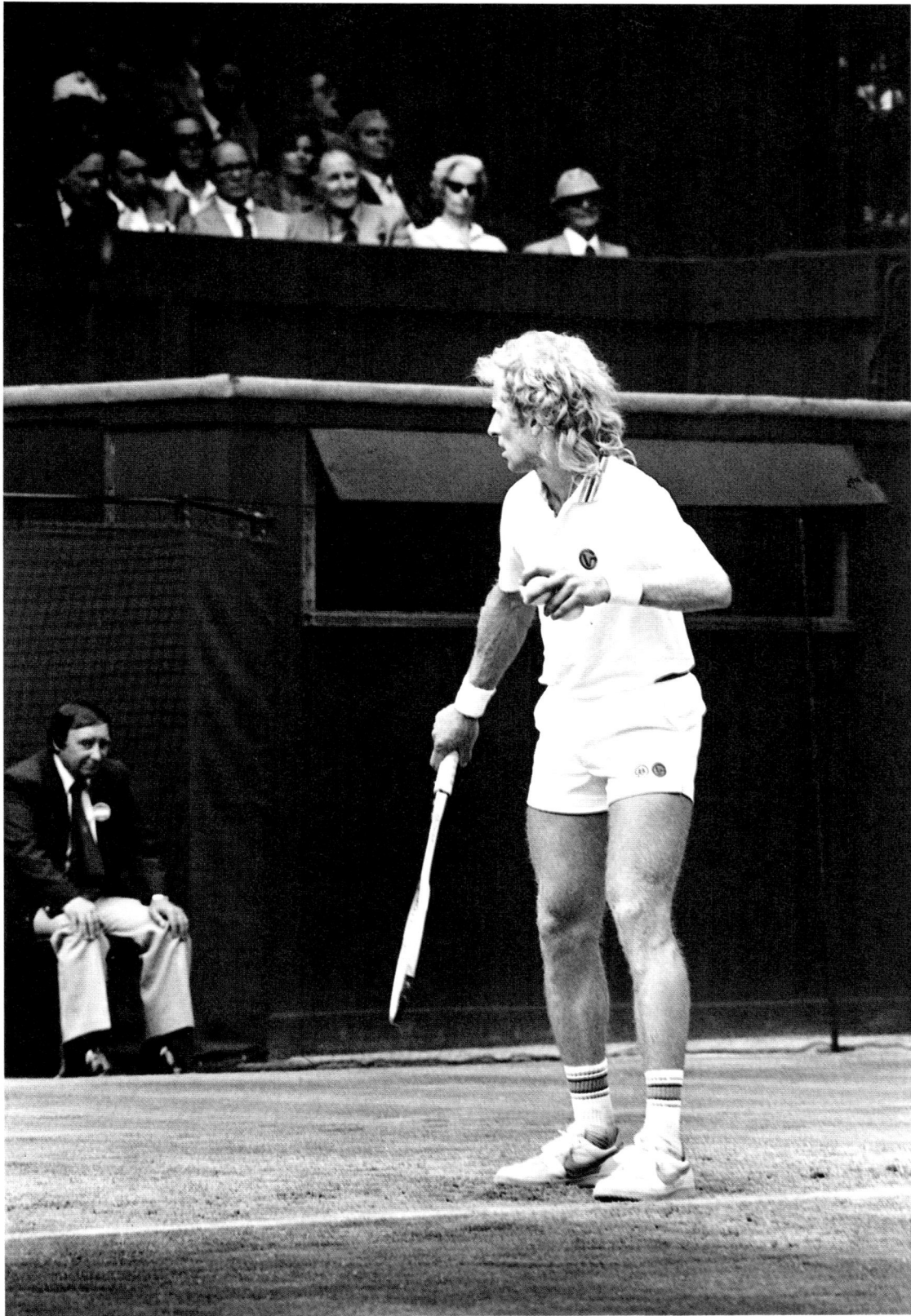

John McEnroe
United States *Wembley 1981*

The serve, like handwriting, swimming or riding a bicycle, is
learned in youth and never forgotten.
Players may add and subtract various ingredients, but the
fundamental action doesn't change.
No coach would ever encourage a pupil to copy John
McEnroe; his position parallel to the baseline is unnecessarily
non-conformist.
But, as he swings around, the body rotation from this angle
will force him upward into the ball.
The result is a fearsome kick which will run away from
the opponent and open up the court for a winning volley.
McEnroe at his best is almost unreturnable. If his serve is not
working well, the rest of his game can seem lightweight.

Yannick Noah
France *Wimbledon 1981*

Noah comes from the Cameroons, so he's black, and French.
Arthur Ashe discovered him on a tour of West Africa in 1971;
shortly afterwards he was brought to France and put into the
French junior tennis machine – whence he emerged at the end
of the seventies full of infinite promise and burdened with
Gallic fantasies about the Four Musketeers and *la gloire*.
Noah's a strong young man, six foot four and finely muscled;
often he plays with a touch that can surprise.
But his professional career has not been free of strain, or his
personal life unclouded.
The French expect a lot from Noah; they have not had a world
champion for generations.
As he starts to serve, all that anxiety surfaces.

Bjorn Borg
Sweden *Wimbledon 1981*

Borg has the look of a man who knows the dangers, and knows what he's doing.
The serve, at this stage, is an unexploded bomb.
When Bjorn was a teenager his serve was strictly so-so.
Then, realising he'd never win Wimbledon without one, he worked on it through several seasons.
Now he's probably the only baseline player who has a better delivery than most serve-volleyers.

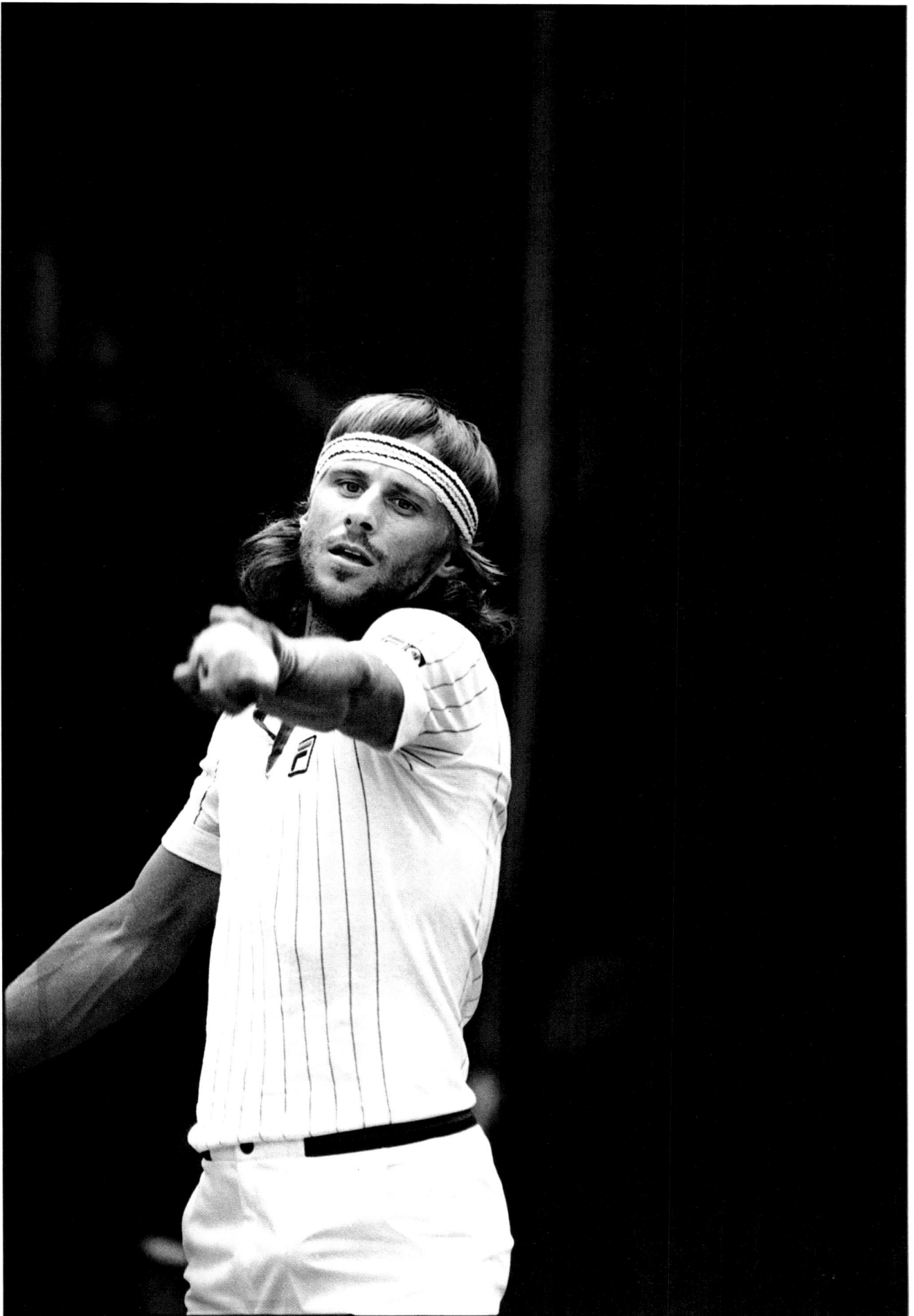

Gene Mayer
United States *Wimbledon 1982*

Mayer's eyes are on the spot where he wants the ball to be long
before it's left his hand.
A pro player will toss the ball into the air millions of times;
he'll know to the split second how he's got to move to hit it
where he wants, with what spin, what force.
Mayer is not one of the game's powerhouse servers. He uses a
Prince racket, with the large head, not considered the ideal
weapon for this purpose.
Nevertheless, he's aware that a male tennis player without a
strong serve is severely handicapped, so his is adequate.
Gene bends his arm on the toss more than most; he's gentling
the ball, as though it was something important and valuable
to him.

Billie Jean King
United States *Birmingham 1982*

Billie Jean's serve was never a thunderbolt, but it was always
accurate and she seldom double faulted.
Her action of placing the ball is precise and elegant.
Because she is a player from the classic past, she holds two
balls in her hand at once.
Modern double-handed girls do not know this trick.

Tracy Austin
United States *Birmingham 1982*

Tracy's going to be overwhelmed by the ball; it's her master.
The serve is an aspect of tennis which remains foreign to Miss
Austin – hers is undoubtedly the worst of any world ranking
player for two decades.
The ball, having consented to be timidly struck, dithers around
and flops exhausted in the opponent's service court. Thence,
it's dispatched by more energetic spirits.
Women's tennis, it's true, does not revolve around service
games, but there's really no excuse for the miserable stuff seen
on championship courts today.

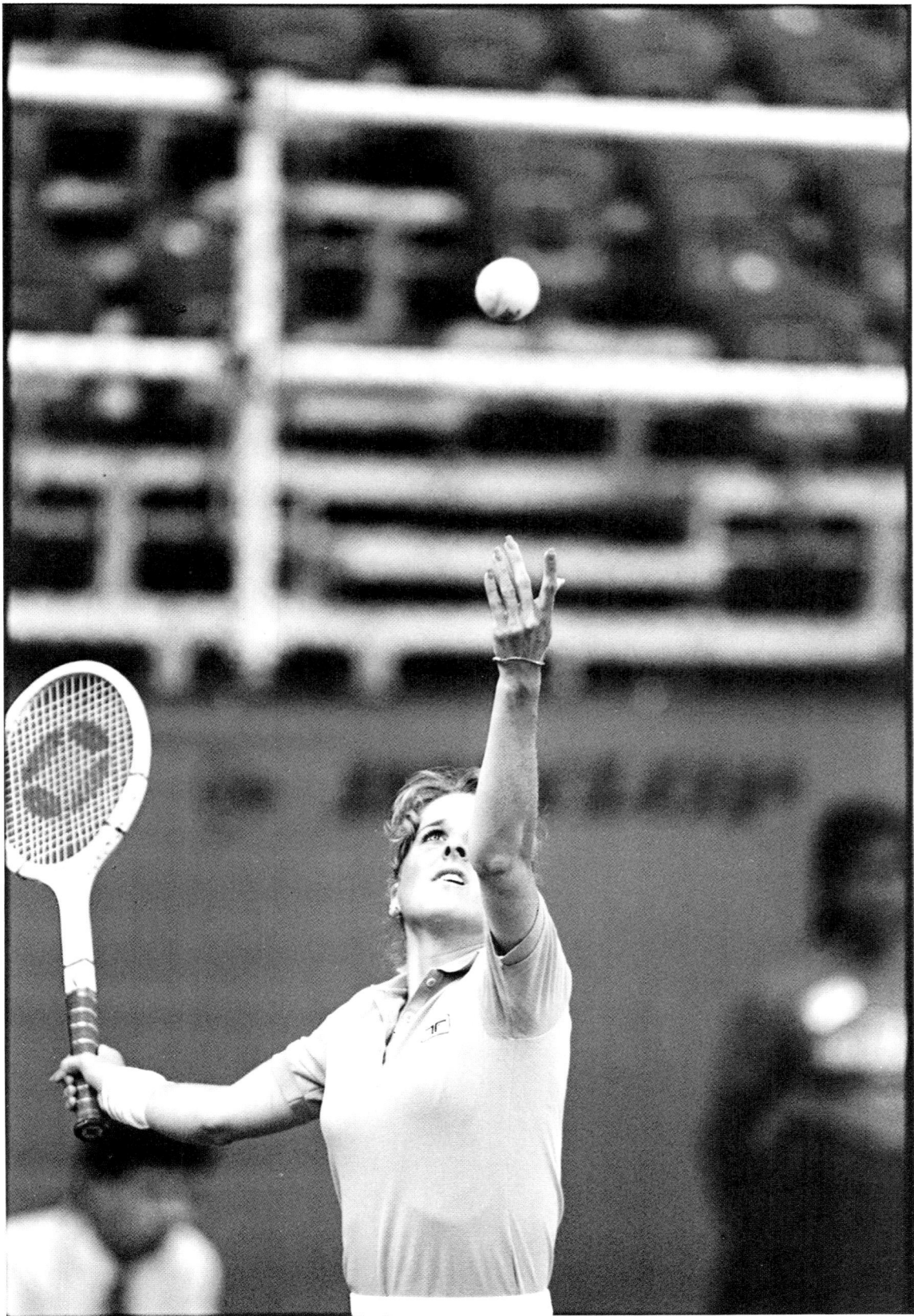

Anne Smith
United States *Wimbledon 1982*

Anne Smith, a dentist's daughter from Texas, is one of those rare women with an excellent serve.
Compare this picture with the one of Tracy Austin. Anne's action is clearly a single flowing movement. Tracy's left and right arm are strangers to each other.
Anne's a medium singles player, a good doubles partner. Her overhead smash is punitive, it's designed to do more than win the point.
Her serve is a more refined version of that shot.
Anne's never bothered about nail polish or pretty frocks; she doesn't apologise for being athletic.

Lloyd Bourne
United States   *Wimbledon 1982*

Bourne's one of a generation of gifted black Americans.
On serve, he's taken individualism about as far as it can go.
This frightful contortion is designed to dislocate rather than
put the ball in play.

Anand Amritraj
India *Birmingham 1982*

Amritraj, of three tennis playing brothers from Madras,
launches himself beyond the point of no return.
This was an indoor tournament; the blackness above and
behind him is appropriately dense. It suggests an empty
universe, a space to be filled by the impact of ball on racket.
After this second, you can only hope.

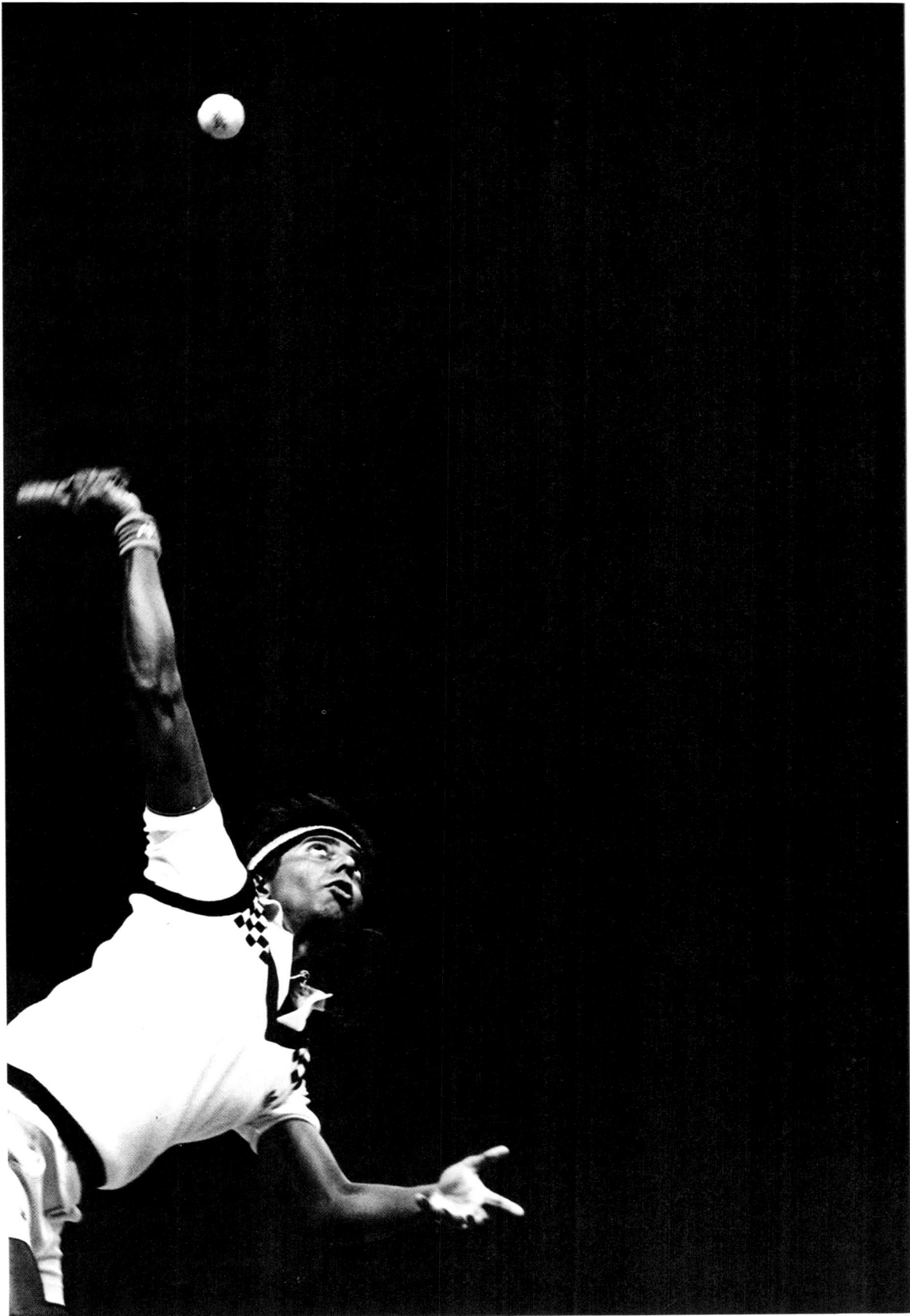

John McEnroe
United States *Wimbledon 1981*

McEnroe has perfected the slice serve. This technique was
briefly considered old-fashioned because of the vogue for
viciously-kicking topspin. So the more homely slice is
re-appearing because few players can handle the complicated
gymnastics of the topspin serve well enough to use it regularly.
The ball is hit with sidespin which makes it curve away on
bouncing. There's a wide margin of error – you can whack
this one and it will still land in court.
John's placed the ball in front of his body and bent his elbow
to breaking point; the racket is prepared to brush across the
ball.
McEnroe's partly responsible for the resurrection of slice.
Some people think of it as a women's shot.
But who wants to fracture their wrists and dislocate their
backs just to be manly?

Ivan Lendl
Czechoslovakia *Wimbledon 1981*

The bomb explodes.

Scenes

Roland Garros
Paris 1982

The French Open Championships are held every spring at the
Stade Roland Garros in the Bois de Boulogne.
It is the epicure's tournament, a distillation of Gallic chic and
Parisian rudeness.
Fans at Roland Garros dress well, eat well, expect to be treated
with courtesy.
This poster for Paris in 1982 was designed by Folon, the
noted Belgian artist. The French windows open from the lines
of a tennis court. The colour is a wash in the reddish-brown
tones of Roland Garros clay.
The choice of Folon, and the sophisticated simplicity of the
poster he produced, sum up tennis in Paris.
Would the committee of the All England Lawn Tennis and
Croquet Club ask David Hockney to design the Wimbledon
programme?

Wimbledon 1981

The use of a wide-angle lens, with its distorting prism, has
linked the two giggling fans, the litter basket and the man
conversing with an unseen friend in a surreal view of this lawn
tennis Mecca.

The gentleman, impeccably dressed and shod, fiddling with
his signet ring, lingers from a bygone social calendar.
Wimbledon once featured in every fashionable diary of the
English Season, sandwiched between horsey Ascot and aquatic
Henley. Now the debs and the debs' delights tend to stay away;
there's too much money in pro tennis, too many pushy agents
and ill-mannered stars.

Pro tennis is *trade*.

Our two girls have come here to gawp at their heroes; they'll
be unlikely to see any Centre Court action because they won't
have been able to afford tickets. Who cares? They're at
Wimbledon.

These kids will have fun anyway; they understand that games
and hero worship properly belong to the very young.

The litter basket simply reminds us that behind the romance
of Wimbledon lies a load of rubbish.

Wimbledon 1982

An Umpire's chair; an English summer.

Heinz Gunthardt Switzerland
Balazcs Taroczy Hungary
Birmingham 1982

The doubles game is an odd adjunct to the main business of
pro tennis. The big stars of today like to save themselves for
the events rich in dollars or prestige, so doubles has been left
to the journeymen who become skilled at the specialised game
and make a good living.

There are tournaments for doubles only: customers like the
fists of fury of good men's doubles; the players enjoy being at
the centre stage instead of the usual sideshow.

Heinz Gunthardt (left) is Swiss and Taroczy Hungarian, a
typically eclectic pairing.

The poetic looking Gunthardt was once touted as a rival to his
contemporary Bjorn Borg but his star has long faded; now he's
just a good player in the ranks and his once straggly blond hair
is as clipped as that of his Hungarian partner.

Taroczy, with the wide forehead of an earnest student, is
Hungary's best professional, but his skills are mostly confined
to clay courts. As a doubles man he's steady and lets
Gunthardt do most of the fireworks.

The combination's successful – the two men won this doubles
event in Birmingham, an indoor production bankrolled by
Texas millionaire and tennis impresario Lamar Hunt.

Both players appear suitably pleased; they've tucked large
cheques into their wallets and are glad to leave the cavernous
barn of the National Exhibition Centre. Behind them the
darkness runs away into an immense grotto. Indoor tennis is
really about making money. Nobody would call these arenas
pleasure domes.

Ball boys *National Exhibition Centre Birmingham 1982*

Indoor tennis edges into theatre, or maybe vaudeville.
These are chorus boys waiting their turn, although the little
fellow on the right, feet neatly tucked into the Third Position,
seems to have more classical things in mind.
Fila, the Italian company, take the opportunity of showering
these boys with designer clothing in the knowledge that their
every movement on court before the television camera will
repay that small investment many thousand-fold.
The boy in the foreground has broken ranks and is wearing the
motif of a French manufacturer on his track suit top, thus
hedging his bets.
Several famous players did duty at one time or another as
ball boys – a chance for the lucky few to come within
expletive distance of their heroes.

Anne Jones
Great Britain *Birmingham 1982*

In a Warwickshire country garden Anne Jones, former
Wimbledon champion, strikes a pose Nicholas Hilliard could
have painted.
She was in charge of the women's tournament being played in
Birmingham, and the script she's consulting is only an order
of play.
There are few such pastoral stops now in the tennis calendar.
Mrs Jones is a Birmingham native, born and bred in the town
and living there.
For many years she was Britain's number one player, far more
deeply English in values and loyalties than Virginia Wade has
ever been.
Mrs Jones beat Billie Jean King to win the women's singles at
Wimbledon in 1969 but the claptrap of fame didn't touch her.
Anne was always your next door neighbour who'd drop in for
a cup of something.